Play and Discover

My BODY

Caryn Jenner

W
FRANKLIN WATTS
LONDON • SYDNEY

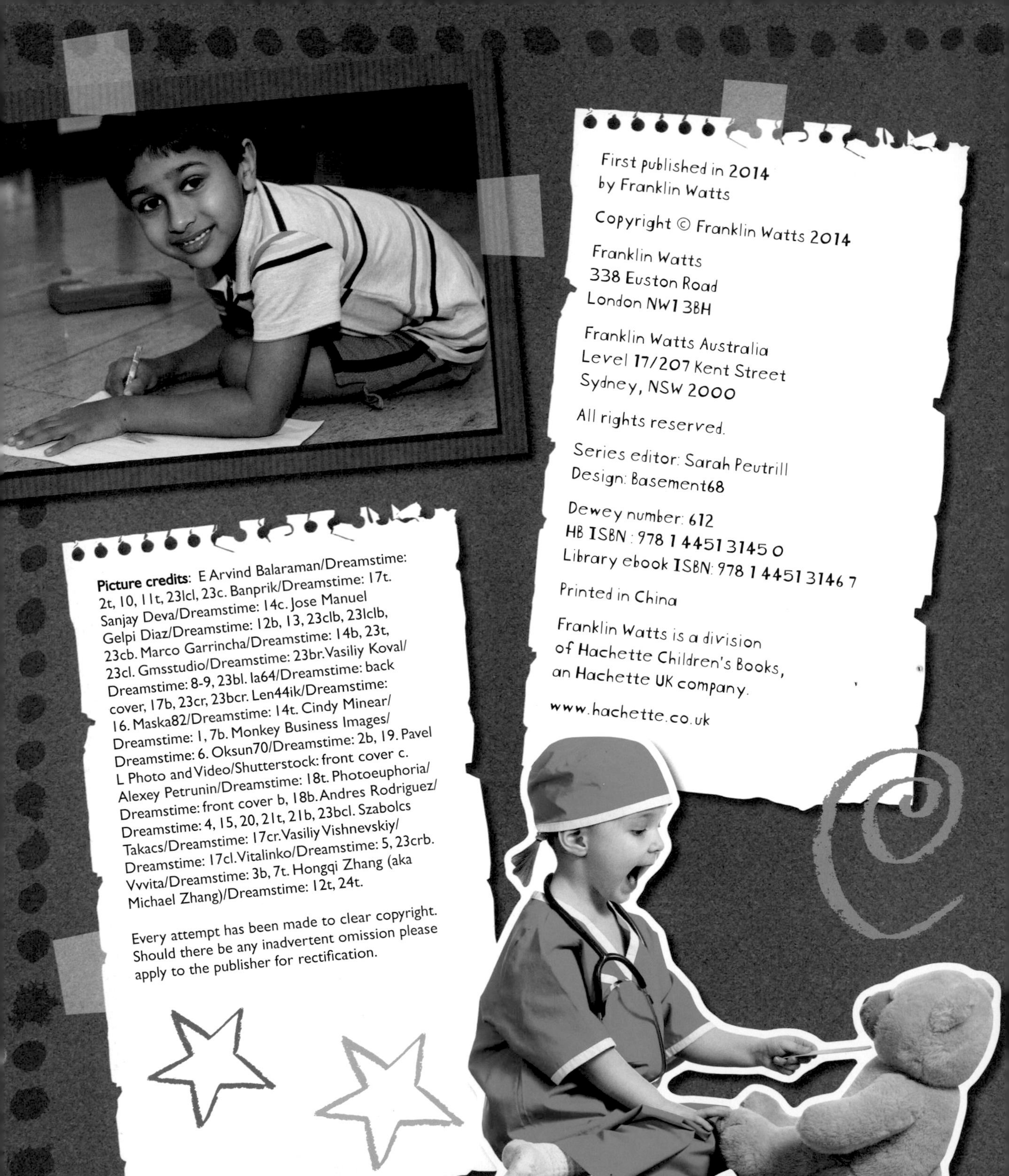

First published in 2014
by Franklin Watts

Franklin Watts
338 Euston Road
London NW1 3BH

Franklin Watts Australia
Level 17/207 Kent Street
Sydney, NSW 2000

Series editor: Sarah Peutrill
Design: Basement68

Dewey number: 612
HB ISBN: 978 1 4451 3145 0
Library ebook ISBN: 978 1 4451 3146 7

Printed in China

Franklin Watts is a division
of Hachette Children's Books,
an Hachette UK company.

www.hachette.co.uk

Picture credits: E Arvind Balaraman/Dreamstime: 2t, 10, 11t, 23lcl, 23c. Banprik/Dreamstime: 17t. Sanjay Deva/Dreamstime: 14c. Jose Manuel Gelpi Diaz/Dreamstime: 12b, 13, 23clb, 23lclb, 23cb. Marco Garrincha/Dreamstime: 14b, 23t, 23cl. Gmsstudio/Dreamstime: 23br. Vasiliy Koval/ Dreamstime: 8-9, 23bl. Ia64/Dreamstime: back cover, 17b, 23cr, 23bcr. Len44ik/Dreamstime: 16. Maska82/Dreamstime: 14t. Cindy Minear/ Dreamstime: 1, 7b. Monkey Business Images/ Dreamstime: 6. Oksun70/Dreamstime: 2b, 19. Pavel L Photo and Video/Shutterstock: front cover c. Alexey Petrunin/Dreamstime: 18t. Photoeuphoria/ Dreamstime: front cover b, 18b. Andres Rodriguez/ Dreamstime: 4, 15, 20, 21t, 21b, 23bcl. Szabolcs Takacs/Dreamstime: 17cr. Vasiliy Vishnevskiy/ Dreamstime: 17cl. Vitalinko/Dreamstime: 5, 23crb. Vvvita/Dreamstime: 3b, 7t. Hongqi Zhang (aka Michael Zhang)/Dreamstime: 12t, 24t.

Contents

Different parts

Hair

Head

My body has lots of different parts.

Arm

Leg

Foot

Eye
Ear
Nose
Mouth
And they all fit together!
Hand
Knee

Which part?
Everyone join in!
Touch your nose.

Touch your head.
Touch your toes.

This is me

This is a picture of me.

I cut it into pieces to make a jigsaw puzzle.
Then I put the puzzle together.
Oops! That's not right!

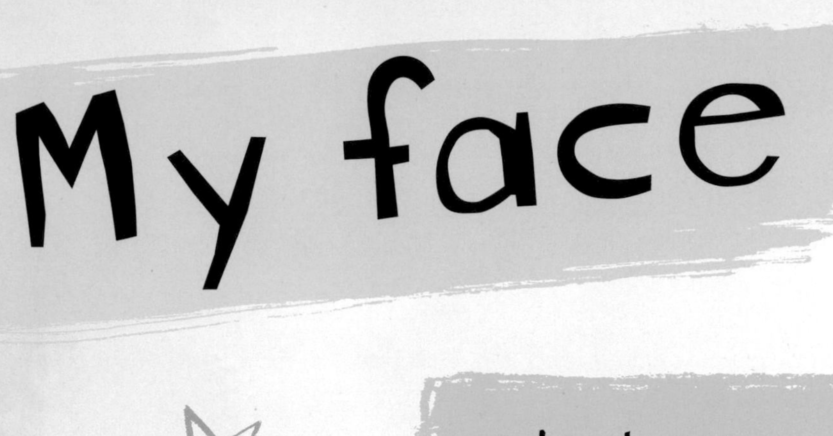

My face

I look at my face in the mirror.

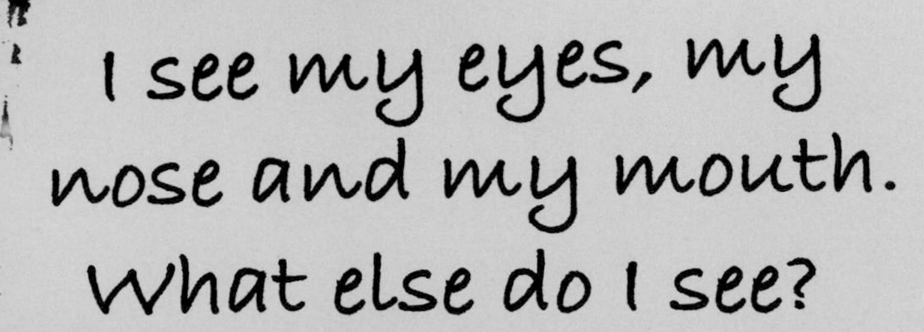

I see my eyes, my nose and my mouth. What else do I see?

Now I draw
a picture
of my face.

Growing

This is me when I was a baby.

This is me when I was two years old.

This is me now. Can you see how I've changed?

Moving

I can jump up high.

I can balance on one leg.

I can stretch up to the sky.

We can run fast.
How can you move your body?

My senses

We're using our senses outside.

We use our hands to feel the sand.

I use my nose to smell a flower.
Tweet, tweet.
I use my ears to hear a bird. Now I use my eyes to spot it!

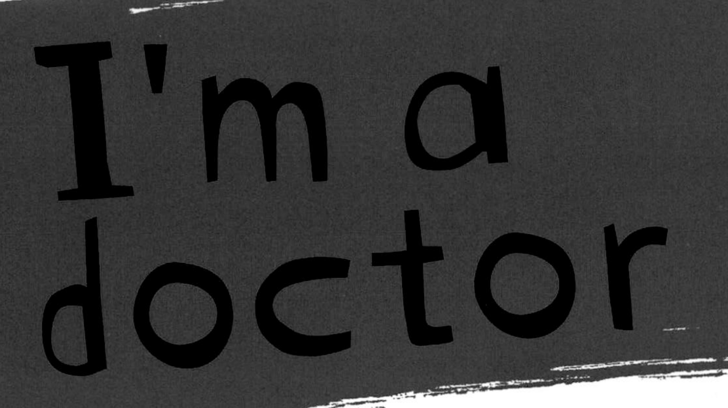

I'm a doctor

This is my doctor's kit. I listen to my teddy's heartbeat.

Thump-thump-thump.

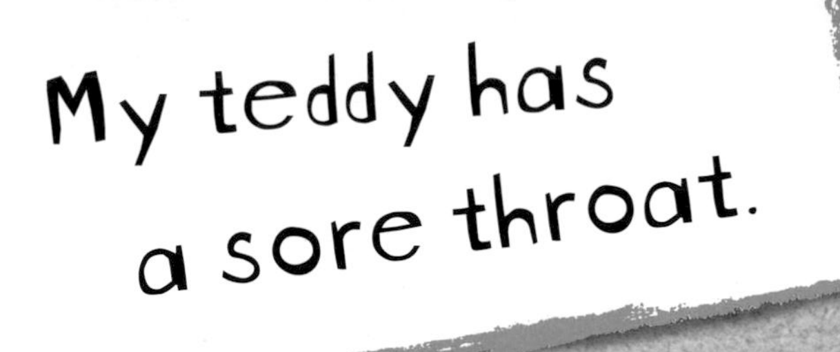
My teddy has
a sore throat.

Open wide, Teddy.
Let me check
it for you.

All about me

This is a book all about me!

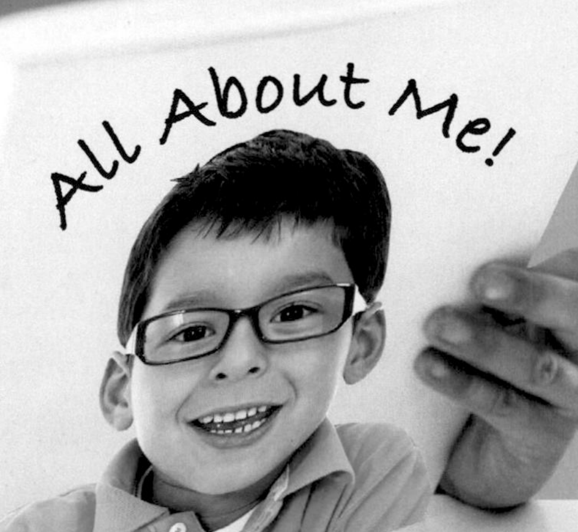

My hair is

My eyes are

I'm this tall.

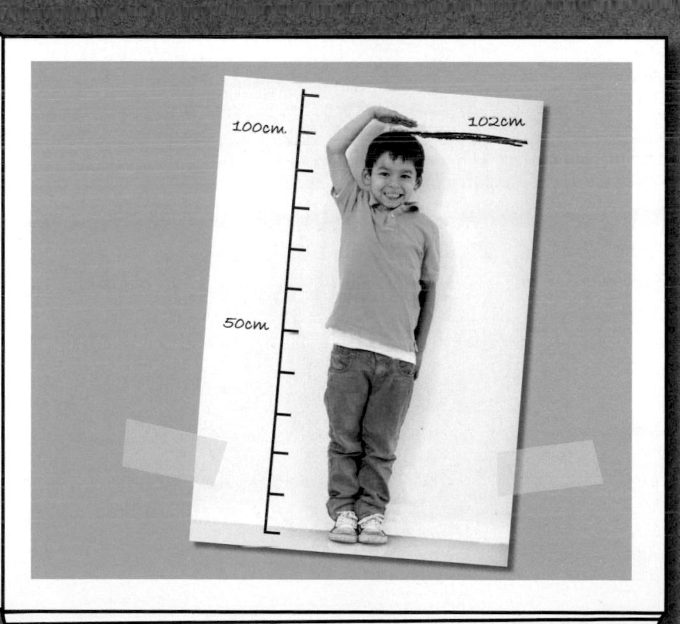

With your friends

Do the Hokey Cokey!

Gather your friends in a circle to sing and dance the Hokey Cokey. Start with a hand, then a foot, then your head and finally your whole self!

You put one hand in. You put one hand out.
In, out, in, out. Shake it all about.
You do the hokey-cokey
and you turn around.
That's what it's all about.
Whoa, the hokey-cokey,
Whoa, the hokey-cokey,
Whoa, the hokey-cokey,
Knees bent, arms stretched, rah, rah, rah!

Word bank

arms

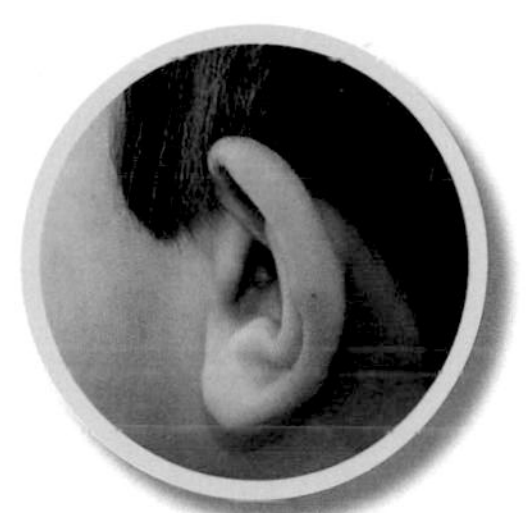
ear

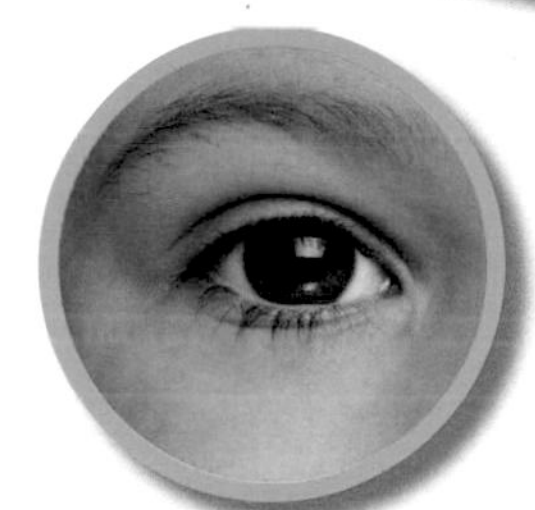
eye

face

feet

hair

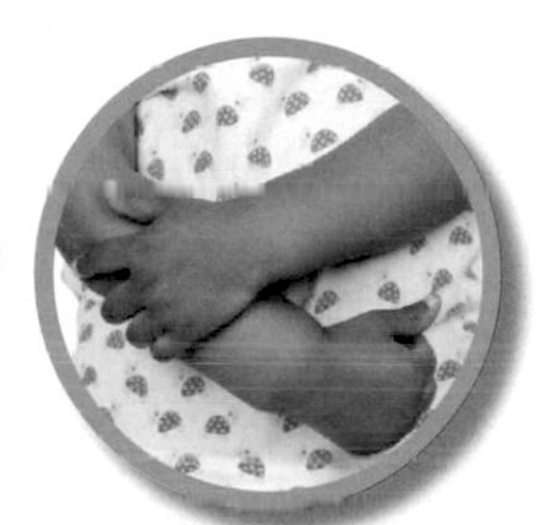
hands

head

legs

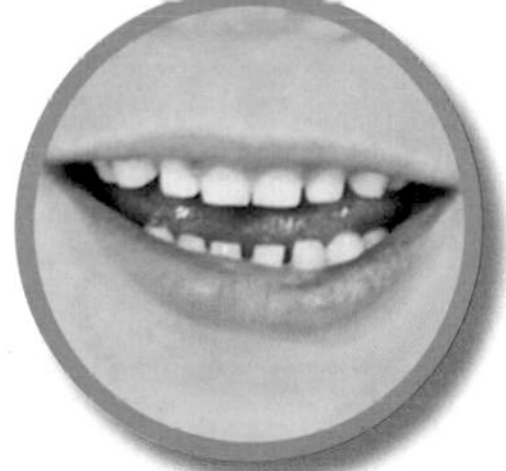
mouth

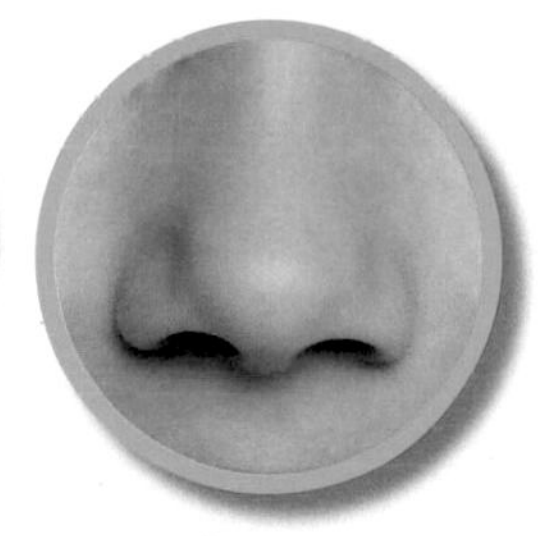
nose

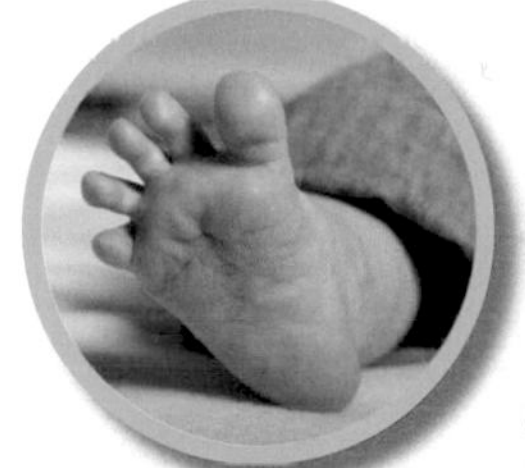
toes

Index

Notes for parents and teachers

Which part? – Play a version of 'Simon Says' that focuses on identifying body parts. Ask the children to touch their nose, head and toes, as in the pictures on pages 6–7. You do it too. Move on to identifying other parts of the body, such as ears, chin and elbow, etc. Let the children take turns to be 'Simon' too.

This is me – Take a full-length photo of each child. They can even make silly poses! If possible, enlarge the photo to A4 size. Glue the photo onto a piece of card and cut it into about six large pieces. Then see if the children can put together the jigsaw puzzle of themselves. Discuss which parts of the body are connected to each other.

My face – Ask the children to study their faces in a mirror. Ask them to name some facial features, such as eyes, nose, mouth, forehead, cheeks and chin. Discuss how everyone's face is unique. (Even identical twins have small differences.) Now have the children draw their own faces, using the mirror for help.

Growing – Ask the children to bring in photos from when they were younger. Discuss how they've changed since then. They've certainly grown taller. What else? Compare what they can do now to what they could do then. They'll also enjoy looking at clothes and shoes from when they were younger.

Moving – Ask the children to take turns to demonstrate different ways that they can move their bodies, using both large motor skills and fine motor skills, from great big jumps to a small nod of the head. You can also take them to the playground and ask them to demonstrate more movements there.

My senses – Encourage the children to practise using their senses. Take them outside and sit in a circle. Ask the children to describe what they see. Then have them close their eyes and ask them to describe what they hear. Let them explore and find things to touch, and describe those too. Can they describe any smells?

I'm a doctor – Teach the children about doctors through role play with a toy doctor's kit. Let the children pretend to be the doctor, while cuddly toys are the patients. For example, the children can pretend to listen to a teddy's heart; bandage a broken arm; check ears, nose and throat; take temperature; or put a plaster on a cut.

All about me – Help the children to make little books about themselves. Include a full-length photo and a close up, with details of hair and eye colour and height. Put the self-portrait from pages 10–11 in the book too. The children can also add photos with their families and doing their favourite activities.